Rabbit's Pajama Party

BY **STUART J. MURPHY**

ILLUSTRATED BY

FRANK REMKIEWICZ

HarperCollinsPublishers

LEVEL
1

To Maureen and Randy and all the pajama parties in their future

—S.J.M.

For Kate and Sarah, who teach in sequence

—F.R.

The illustrations in this book were done in watercolor and Prismacolors on Bristol paper.

HarperCollins®, ■®, and MathStart® are trademarks of HarperCollins Publishers Inc. For more information about the MathStart Series, please write to HarperCollins Children's Books, 195 Broadway, New York, NY 10007, or visit our web site at http://www.harperchildrens.com.

Bugs incorporated in the MathStart series design were painted by Jon Buller.

Rabbit's Pajama Party
Text copyright © 1999 by Stuart J. Murphy
Illustrations copyright © 1999 by Frank Remkiewicz
Manufactured in China. All rights reserved.
Library of Congress Cataloging-in-Publication Data
Murphy, Stuart J., date
    Rabbit's pajama party / by Stuart J. Murphy ; illustrated by Frank Remkiewicz.
       p.   cm. — (MathStart)
    "Level 1, sequencing."
    Summary: A group of animal friends have fun at a pajama party while demonstrating activities that happen in a particular order or sequence.
    ISBN 0-06-027616-9. — ISBN 0-06-027617-7 (lib. bdg.).
    ISBN 0-06-446722-8 (pbk.)
    1. Sequences (Mathematics)—Juvenile literature.
[1. Sequences (Mathematics)]   I. Remkiewicz, Frank, ill.
II. Title.   III. Series.
QA292.M87   1999   98-36617
515'.24—dc21   CIP
                                                     AC

Typography by Michele N. Tupper
16 17 SCP 20 19
❖

Rabbit's Pajama Party

My pajama party is about to begin!

I run to the door and let my friends in.

We gobble our dinner,
pizza with cheese,

9

and slurp down our fruit juice,
as much as we please.

10

For dessert we make sundaes,
hot fudge and whipped cream,

12

with a cherry on top—
an elephant's dream.

14

Then Mom says,
"It's time to get ready for bed."

17

So we pull on our pj's—
mine are bright red.

19

When everyone's ready,
Mom says, "All right!"

"Now into your sleeping bags.
Zip them up tight."

Elephant giggles,
and I start to laugh!

Mom takes one last picture.
"Good night!" shouts Giraffe.

But the fun has just started.
We don't want to rest.

29

We tell scary stories—
the kind we like best.

There's a "Boo,"
then a scream
and a "Shhhh,"
then a roar.

But after a while
all I hear
is Mouse snore.

letting friends in

eating dinner

making sundaes

putting on pj's

getting into sleeping bags

saying good night

What Happened at Rabbit's Pajama Party

33

FOR ADULTS AND KIDS

In *Rabbit's Pajama Party*, the math concept presented is time sequencing. Understanding what comes first, what comes next, what happens after that, and what happens last is important in the development of a child's understanding of mathematics as well as story comprehension.

If you would like to have more fun with the math concepts presented in *Rabbit's Pajama Party*, here are a few suggestions:

• Read the story with the child and describe what is going on in each picture. Ask, "What do you think will happen next?"

• While reading the story, point out the sequence of events in the pictures. Encourage the child to tell the story using the words "first," "next," "then," and "last."

• After reading the story, ask, "What happened first?" "What happened next?" "Then what happened?" "What was the last thing that happened?"

• Make a timeline for the story. For example, at 5:00 the friends arrive, at 6:00 they eat pizza, and so on.

• Together, discuss events that require steps in a particular order or sequence—for example, making a peanut-butter-and-jelly sandwich. Write down the steps as the child dictates them and then make the sandwich, following the steps exactly. If they are not in the correct sequence, discuss what went wrong and make corrections.

Following are some activities that will help you extend the concepts presented in *Rabbit's Pajama Party* into a child's life:

Sleepover Party: Plan a sleepover party (real or make-believe). Discuss whom to invite. Make a list of the activities for the party and write each activity, or ask the child to draw a picture of each activity, on a note card. Then help the child place the pictures in order to show the sequence of events.

Cartoons: Clip out a favorite comic strip from the newspaper. Cut the comic strip into separate frames and ask the child to place the pieces in the right sequence.

Games: Decide on a game that you want to play. As you're playing, talk about the sequence of events involved. What happens first? Then what happens? What would happen if you tried to play the game out of sequence?

The following stories include concepts similar to those that are presented in *Rabbit's Pajama Party:*

- BY THE DAWN'S EARLY LIGHT by Karen Ackerman
- GROWING VEGETABLE SOUP by Lois Ehlert
- PEANUT BUTTER AND JELLY: *A Play Rhyme* by Nadine Bernard Westcott

35